**Shanmuganathan Vasanthapriyan**
**R.B.T. Bhagya**
**Prasad M. Jayaweera**

**Collaboration Modelling Framework for Legal Workflow Management**

AF167900

Shanmuganathan Vasanthapriyan
R.B.T. Bhagya
Prasad M. Jayaweera

# Collaboration Modelling Framework for Legal Workflow Management

## Collaboration modelling framework for Courts Hearing Workflow Specification for Sri Lankan Context

**LAP LAMBERT** Academic Publishing

**Impressum / Imprint**

Bibliografische Information der Deutschen Nationalbibliothek: Die Deutsche Nationalbibliothek verzeichnet diese Publikation in der Deutschen Nationalbibliografie; detaillierte bibliografische Daten sind im Internet über http://dnb.d-nb.de abrufbar.
Alle in diesem Buch genannten Marken und Produktnamen unterliegen warenzeichen-, marken- oder patentrechtlichem Schutz bzw. sind Warenzeichen oder eingetragene Warenzeichen der jeweiligen Inhaber. Die Wiedergabe von Marken, Produktnamen, Gebrauchsnamen, Handelsnamen, Warenbezeichnungen u.s.w. in diesem Werk berechtigt auch ohne besondere Kennzeichnung nicht zu der Annahme, dass solche Namen im Sinne der Warenzeichen- und Markenschutzgesetzgebung als frei zu betrachten wären und daher von jedermann benutzt werden dürften.

Bibliographic information published by the Deutsche Nationalbibliothek: The Deutsche Nationalbibliothek lists this publication in the Deutsche Nationalbibliografie; detailed bibliographic data are available in the Internet at http://dnb.d-nb.de.
Any brand names and product names mentioned in this book are subject to trademark, brand or patent protection and are trademarks or registered trademarks of their respective holders. The use of brand names, product names, common names, trade names, product descriptions etc. even without a particular marking in this works is in no way to be construed to mean that such names may be regarded as unrestricted in respect of trademark and brand protection legislation and could thus be used by anyone.

Coverbild / Cover image: www.ingimage.com

Verlag / Publisher:
LAP LAMBERT Academic Publishing
ist ein Imprint der / is a trademark of
OmniScriptum GmbH & Co. KG
Heinrich-Böcking-Str. 6-8, 66121 Saarbrücken, Deutschland / Germany
Email: info@lap-publishing.com

Herstellung: siehe letzte Seite /
Printed at: see last page
ISBN: 978-3-659-60847-6

# Collaboration Modelling Framework for Legal Workflow Management

Authors:

S. Vasanthapriyan & R.P.T. Bhagya
Department of Computing & Information Systems
Sabaragamuwa University of Sri Lanka
Sri Lanka

P. Jayaweera
Department of Computer Science
University of Sri Jayewardenepura
Sri Lanka

# Abstract

Effectiveness and efficiency of the legal sector are highly relying on the coordination of collaborative workflow activities to cope with highly dynamic and complex information exchanges among many different partners. For instance most of the prevailing courts procedures are with huge efficiency and productivity issues where not only legal service recipients but also supporting auxiliary parties heavily suffering besides huge resource wastages. In the context of ever increasing number of legal cases and roles offering different legal services, we have discovered the appropriateness of the adaptation of Workflow Management Systems in legal sector to address the resulting complexities and performance issues in legal service collaborations. In this work, a Legal Collaboration Modeling Framework has been introduced with the objective of facilitating the foundational requirement, i.e. specification of legal workflows, for setting up workflow systems in legal sector. In the proposed framework, a set of primitive transaction patterns have been de-veloped in align with UN/CEFACT's transaction patterns proposal for generic business collaboration modeling. The two main contributions of this work are a collaboration modeling framework and application areas of the framework in district courts legal process modeling. The proposed framework was semantically rich enough for composing complex multi-party legal collaborations with promising results in workflow coordination. The applications of the modeling framework resulted possibility of streamlining and then to ensure coordination among workflow activities to achieve productivity and efficiency.

Keywords: Workflow Management, Legal Workflow, Legal Collaboration Modeling, Transaction Patterns

# Contents

# List of Figures

# 1

# Introduction

This chapter presents the background objectives and motivation of the research, and the work completed in respect to the development of Legal Collaboration Modeling Framework.

## 1.1 Research Motivation

The legal sector is one of the largest single industries all over the world. Mainly, it comprises with a diverse array of legal professionals such as judges, attorneys, court clerks, court reporters etc. and also outsiders such as plaintiffs, defendants, witnesses etc.

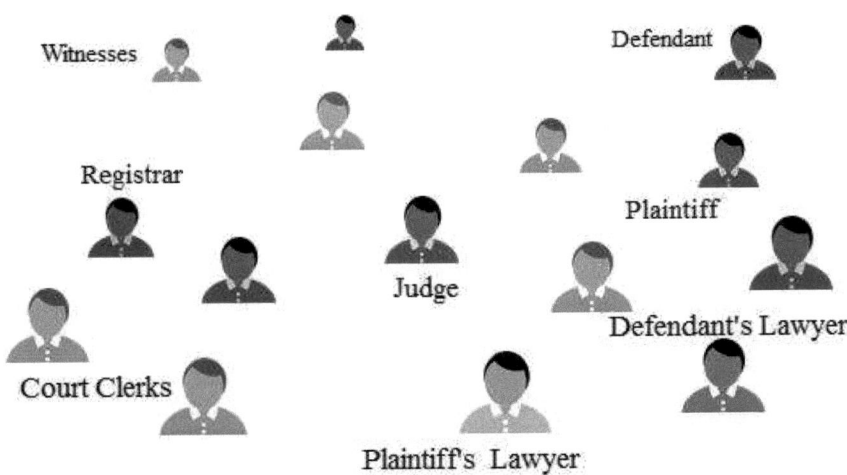

Figure 1.1: Legal Sector Composition

Usually, these sector participants are belong to diverse domains and dispersed around many geographical areas while acting on same legal cases. However, any work performed by one partner is utmost importance to all others in order to deliver high quality legal services. Hence, each participant in the legal sector needs to collaborate with each other to share case related information in order to deliver cost effective and best professionally practiced legal services, which in turn gives rise to highly dynamic and complex information exchanges.

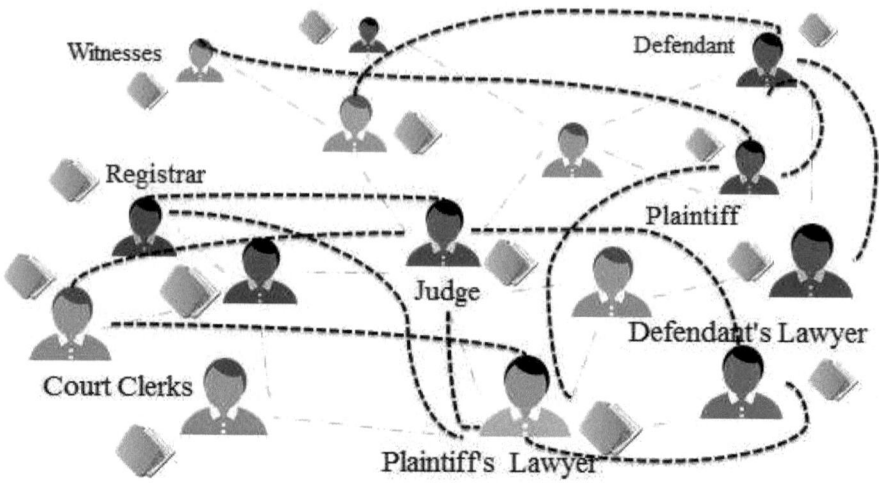

Figure 1.2: Information Exchanges among Participants

However, frequently created new legal cases and increased numbers of roles offering different legal services are the prominent factors, worsening the aforementioned situations.

One of the popular attempts to solve these complexities and performance issues in legal service collaborations is the introduction of Workflow Management (WFM) into legal sector for the coordination of various flows of legal information exchanges among the participants. A Workflow Management System (WFMS) supports design, execution and monitoring of general long-lasting business processes that typically involve multiple activities and multiple collaborating parties in a distributed environment[7]. By formalizing the workflow activities, WFMSs promise to increase the efficiency of business processes and, consequently, to raise the productivity of an organization. It therefore is clear that, the adaptation of WFMS in legal sector could lead to overcome the complexity issues in multi-party collaboration, while enabling more efficient functionalities and improving the quality of legal services.

The designing of WFMS consists of several steps and among them, development of a workflow model and generating the workflow specification is widely accepted as the prominent major stage. In general, a clear workflow model paves a way to an accurate implementation of workflow system functions. In the process of workflow modeling, different aspects such as value, goal and collaborations should be considered. This will help to structure the modeling process on a solid basis. Currently, there are several modeling methodologies for business process and workflow process modeling with the focus of supporting the business collaboration and the structure of information exchanges. For instance, in electronic business designing, UN/CEFACT's (United Nation's Center for Trade Facilitation and Electronic Business) recommendations could be considered as a globally accepted standard.

However during our literature survey, it was evident that there are no much established and widely adopted contributions to be adopted in the legal sector that could assist in modeling the legal workflows for defining the choreography for legal sector collaborations with the objective of facilitating legal collaborations modeling for initiating legal WFMS. Accordingly, this study tries to find an answer to the unavailability of systematic modeling methodology to support legal service solution developments.

## 1.2   Research Purpose

The overall purpose of this research work can be described as an effort to facilitate the modeling of legal service collaboration workflows. Hence, this research study aims to investigate the existing business collaboration modeling standards and then to develop a framework for modeling legal service collaborations while identifying the related activities, services and business concepts in the legal sector. The modeling framework would help to understand the legal service collaboration processes as well as to facilitate the collaboration modeling in legal domain, in such a way as to provide a useful input for the creation of legal WFMS to foster excellence legal services and to facilitate whole of sector collaborations.

## 1.3   Research Methodologies

In the broadest sense, the definition of a research includes any gathering of data, information and facts for the advancement of knowledge. General aims of a research are to observe and describe, predict, determination of the causes and to explain the findings. Accordingly, it is necessary to develop a research methodology to achieve the targeted goal and objectives of any research work.

Information and Communication Systems (ICS) research [2] are basically carried out in two complementary paradigms: design science and behavioral science. The behavioral science research paradigm has its roots in natural science research methods. It seeks to develop and justify theories that explain or predict organizational and human phenomena surrounding the analysis, design, implementation, management, and use of information systems. Such theories ultimately inform researchers and practitioners of the interactions among people, technology, and organizations that must be managed if an information system is to achieve its stated purpose, namely improving the effectiveness and efficiency of an organization. These theories impact and are impacted by design decisions made with respect to the system development methodology used and the functional capabilities, information contents, and human interfaces implemented within the information system.

On the other hand, design science paradigm [2] has its roots in engineering and the sciences of the artificial. It is fundamentally a problem solving paradigm. It seeks to create innovations that define the ideas, practices, technical capabilities, and products through which the analysis, design, implementation, management, and use of information systems can be effectively and efficiently accomplished. Such artifacts are not exempt from natural laws or behavioral theories. To the contrary, their creation relies on existing kernel theories that are applied, tested, modified, and extended through the experience, creativity, intuition, and problem solving capabilities of the researcher.

There are several other possible categorizations on popular research methodologies. Commonly available categorization scheme for research work in sciences and humanities is called Quantitative Research vs. Qualitative Research [2]. Quantitative research is a more logical and data-led approach which provides a measure of what people think from a statistical and numerical point of view. Quantitative research can gather a large amount of data that can be easily organized and manipulated into reports for analysis. Unlike quantitative research which relies on numbers and data, qualitative research is more focused on how people feel, what they think and why they make certain choices. For qualitative researching, grounded theory and action research are two widely known approaches. Put simply, action research is learning by doing; a group of people identify a problem, do something to resolve it, see how successful their efforts were, and if not satisfied, try again.

Action research [2] aims to contribute both to the practical concerns of people in an immediate problematic situation and to further the goals of social science simultaneously. Thus, there is a dual commitment in action research to study a system and concurrently to collaborate with members of the system in changing it in what is together regarded as a desirable direction. Accomplishing this twin goal requires the active collaboration of researcher and client, and thus it stresses the importance of co-learning as a primary aspect of the research process.

Generally, by using appropriate research methods, knowledge should be gathered first. Given below are the research methods which commonly used for information gathering in ICS based research [2].

- Speculation - rely on the knowledge and experience of the persons carrying out the research

- Case Study - a single phenomenon is studied in depth in a certain organizational setting

- Literature Analysis - existing literature are criticized, analyzed and extended in order to build new foundation

- Survey - data are captured from individuals using predefined and structured questionnaires

- Field Study - a single or multiple phenomenon is studied in single or multiple organizational settings

- Laboratory Experiment - researches are conducted in laboratory environments by controlling the various experimental variables involved

- Secondary Data - use already collected data

- Interview: Research conducted by collecting information by interviewing people

However, based on the research purpose, the approach that we took for the development process of our solution could be considered as a hybrid of methodological approach. The said hybrid methodology is based on three phases Analysis phase, Development phase and Evaluation phase. Under Analysis phase, a depth literature survey was conducted on the related projects available for legal solution developments and UN/CEFACT's Modeling Methodology (UMM) standards for business domain. Next, the concepts of the court system were studied by discussing with the experts in legal sector. Here, by taking current divorce case procedure in civil case category under districts court system in Sri Lanka as an example; we have studied the case workflows in order to identify the associated process activities and performers. We have surveyed a number of best practice divorce cases around the country by visiting district courts in order to collect data on divorce case proceedings. Then, using the design science research method, gathered knowledge was applied to develop the modeling framework. Finally, the proposed modeling framework was evaluated with domain experts under the evaluation phase.

The remainder of the book is arranged into four main sections. First provides the back-ground on related aspects. Then a set of transaction patterns for legal collaboration modeling are introduced and the applications of district courts legal workflow specification with a brief evaluation are presented. Finally, the work concludes with summary conclusions are drawn.

# 2

# Workflow Management Overview

In this chapter some of the bases on workflow management are explained. This context will make it easier for the reader to understand this research work.

## 2.1   Workflow Management

A business process is one focused upon the production of particular products. These may be either physical products or an assessment. On the other hand, a workflow could be defined as a collection of tasks organized to accomplish some business process. Such a task can be performed by one or a team of human, or one or more software systems, or a combination of these.

The term WFM [7] refers to the ideas, methods, techniques, and software used to support structured business processes. The objective of WFM is to achieve streamlined and easy-to-maintain work processes. Accordingly, WFM involves everything from modeling workflows up to synchronizing the activities of information systems and humans that perform the workflows. In particular, management of a workflow includes the following:

- Workflow modeling and specification - requires workflow models and methodologies for capturing a process as a workflow specification

- Process reengineering - requires methodologies for optimizing the process

- Workflow implementation and automation - requires methodologies and technology for using information systems, and human performers to implement, schedule, execute and control the workflow tasks as described by the workflow specification

Managing workflow appropriately is an important component of a business for a variety of reasons. The primary advantage to WFM is improved efficiency within the business. By automating many of the processes within a business and establishing a procedure that is consistently followed, unnecessary steps are eliminated, and every member of the team is fully aware of his or her responsibilities. This method also makes it easier to track employee and machine performance. When a link in the chain is broken, it is simple to go back and determine where this occurred. In addition, WFM serves to standardize working methods, ensuring that every employee working on the same level is performing the same function. WFM also helps businesses find ways to improve their production process. By streamlining the responsibilities of each employee and clarifying the roles of every employee and machine within the process, the organization can more easily determine where improvements can be made to increase efficiency and to improve the quality of the service.

By using specialized workflow applications, businesses also enjoy increased flexibility. By tracking processes with software and inputting various alternative scenarios, the organization can more easily determine viable options for improvement. In addition, the software can be used to examine one small component of workflow or workflow at the company-wide level. This is particularly helpful to large businesses that may have several offices spread throughout the country.

## 2.2 Workflow Management Systems

WFMS [7] are designed to support business processes. Business process consists of a number of activities that can be executed manually, automatically or using a combination of these two. A WFMS does not only support the execution of activities, but also takes care of the distribution and assignment of work items to employees, and provides the possibility to keep track of cases and to gain statistics of the process and the workers. The execution of these tasks is based on a workflow model or a workflow specification.

### 2.2.1 Workflow Management Reference Model

The Workflow Management Coalition (WFMC) [7] has developed a workflow management reference model in order to create a general framework for the development of workflow management applications. The reference model indicates the major components and interfaces of a workflow management system.

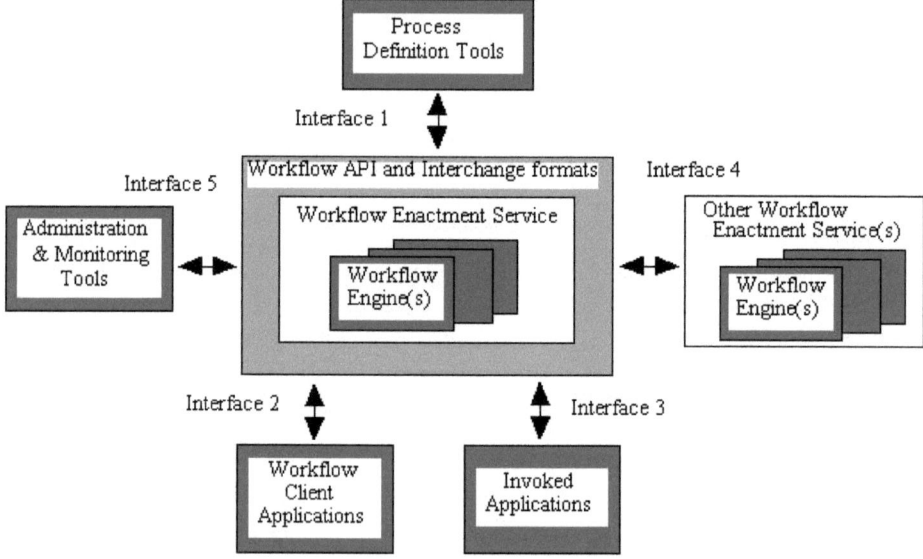

Figure 2.1: Reference Model

**Workflow Enactment Service**

The workflow enactment service is the core of a WFMS. The WFMC defines the workflow enactment service as a software service that may consist of one or more workflow engines in order to create, manage and execute a workflow process. It creates new cases, generates work items based upon the workflow specification, matches resources and work items, supports the performance of activities, and enables the recording of particular aspects of the workflow, means that the workflow enactment service ensures that the right activities are carried out in the right order and by the right people.

**Interfaces**

The workflow enactment service manages the workflow process at runtime. In order to perform the process, the workflow enactment service interfaces with other components.

- Process definition tool - A workflow engine operates based on one or more workflow specifications. In the workflow reference model, the tools for constructing these workflow specifications are known as process definition tools.

- Workflow client applications - Those employees who are only involved in the actual execution of a workflow process will never use the process definition tools. The only contact they have with the WFMS is through the workflow client applications. Each employee has a worklist, which forms part of the workflow client applications. The workflow engine uses this worklist to show which work items need to be carried out.

- Invoked applications - The performing of an activity may result in the starting up of one or more applications. These do not form a part of the WFMS because they are associated with the actual performance of work, not to its logistical management. Such applications do belong to the workflow system. These applications can be fully automatic applications or interactive applications.

- Other workflow enactment services - A workflow system may contain several workflow engines. These come under the same management and use the same workflow definitions. Besides, it is also possible to link several autonomous workflow systems with one another.

- Administration and monitoring tools - The workflow enactment service ensures the processing of cases based upon workflow definitions. The supervision and operational management of these flows are done using administration and monitoring tools. These can be divided into tools for operational management of the workflows and tools for recording and reporting.

## 2.3 Workflow Management System Development

Based on the WFMC reference model, the highest level development architecture of a WFMS could be characterized into build-time and run-time functions. The build-time functions are concerned with defining and modeling workflow activities; while the run-time functions are concerned with managing the workflow execution and interactions with resources for processing workflow applications.

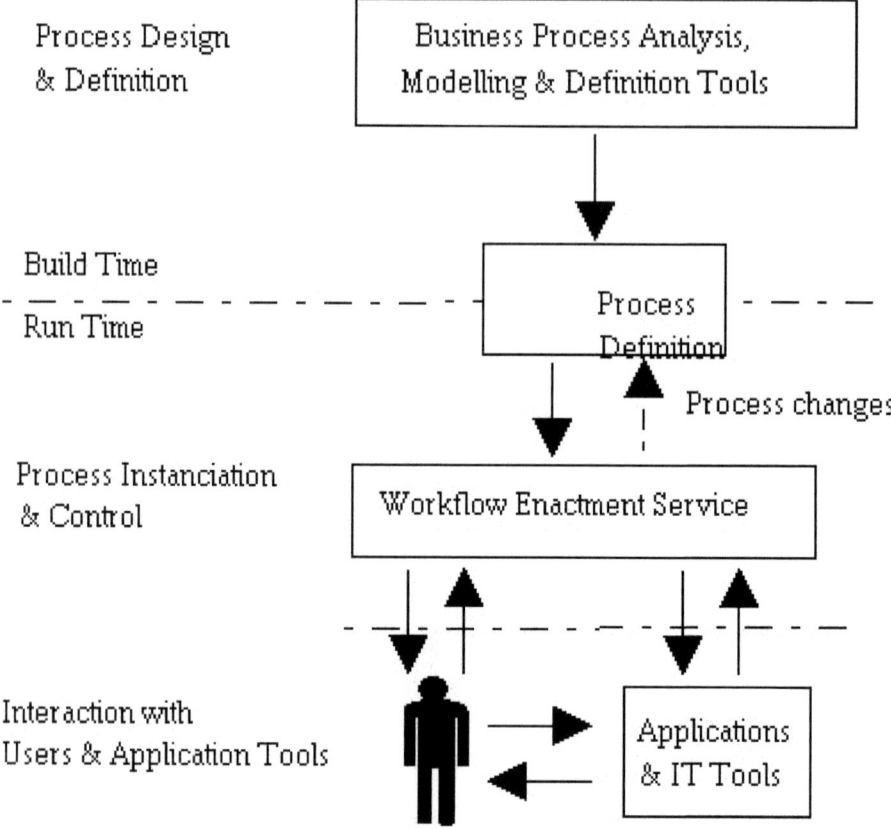

Figure 2.2: High Level Development Architecture

Accordingly, users of a WFMS interact with workflow modeling methodologies and techniques to generate a workflow specification, which is then made available to a run-time service called workflow enactment service for execution.

### 2.3.1 Specification of Workflows

A workflow specification is a computerized representation of a workflow process. Usually, a workflow specification captures a workflow abstraction. The workflow abstraction level in a workflow specification depends on the intended use of the workflow specification. For example, a workflow specification may describe a process at the highest conceptual level necessary for understanding, evaluating, and redesigning the process. On the other hand, another workflow specification may describe the same process at a low level of detail required for performing workflow implementation.

Generally, to build up a workflow specification requires a workflow model. We can refer such workflow model as a static representation of a workflow process. A workflow model typically includes a set of concepts that are useful to describe processes, their tasks, the dependencies among tasks, and the required roles that can perform the specified tasks.

Constructing a workflow model is not an easy task. Our investigations have shown that the hardest task in the development of a workflow model is how to relate it with the concepts and the notations that are truthful to a specific domain. More importantly, to describe the structure, behavior, and properties of discourse of interest, a special modeling methodology that is capable of describing the language of these models is required.

## 2.4   Legal Workflow Management Systems

WFMS are designed to improve the workflow processes by providing technology to automate different aspects of processes by routing work in the proper sequence, providing access to data and documents required by the individual work performers, and tracking all aspects of the process execution. Accordingly, this approach is particularly valuable when streamlining the work coordination in legal sector to enable more efficient functionalities and improve the quality of service as the partners within the sector are initially dispersed around many geographical areas while acting on the same case.

Currently, there are several modeling standards for generic business workflow modeling with the focus of supporting business collaborations. However during our literature survey, it was evident that there is no any work to be adopted in legal sector that could assist in modeling legal collaboration workflows. Hence, our work focused on the development of a meta-modeling framework for legal service collaboration modeling which includes the main semantics of modeling elements with the objective of facilitating the legal collaboration modeling to generate legal workflow service specifications. Correspondingly, related framework development efforts are described in the following chapters.

# 3

# Domain Analysis

In order to design a universal modeling framework that is practical and usable, we have to study the domain. Such main foundation of our work is introduced in this chapter. The chapter starts with a brief survey of some common actors involved in case proceedings and ends with an explanation of how divorce case workflow at the district court happens in general. Taking current divorce case procedure in civil case category under districts court system in Sri Lanka as example; we have studied the case workflow in order to identify the associated process activities and performers. We have surveyed a number of best practice divorce cases around the country by visiting district courts in order to collect data on divorce case proceedings.

## 3.1 Involving Parties

There are many people involved in the court system. Below is a list of the people identified through the domain analysis.

- Judge - A person invested with judicial power.

- Associate Judge - A person invested with limited judicial powers within the Civil jurisdiction of the Court, who adjudicates interim matters in court cases.

- Associate - An Officer of the Court. Sits in front of the Judge or Associate Judge and assists in the administration of the Court. Any documents produced under subpoena should be given to the Associate.

- Tipstaff - An Officer of the Court. Sits next to the Associate and in front of the Judge. He or she is responsible for keeping order in the Court and will usually swear in or affirm the witness.

- Plaintiff - The person who brings a civil proceeding.

- Defendant The person against whom a civil proceeding is brought.

- Plaintiff's barrister - A lawyer employed by the plaintiff to represent him or her in Court. The barrister will usually wear robes and a wig and will face the Judge.

- Plaintiff's solicitor - A lawyer employed by the plaintiff, who prepares the papers for the barrister and who sits at the Bar table opposite the barrister in Court.

- Defendant's Barrister - A lawyer employed by the defendant to represent him or her in Court. The barrister will usually wear robes and a wig and will face the Judge.

- Defendant's solicitor - A lawyer employed by the defendant, who prepares the papers for the barrister and who sits at the Bar table opposite the barrister in Court.

- Witness - A person called to give evidence on behalf of one of the parties.

## 3.2 Divorce Case Workflow

When developing a framework for modeling complex multi-party legal service collaborations with the objective of facilitating the foundational requirement for setting up a WFMS, we have to understand the domain requirements initially.

The Marriage Registration Ordinance and the Civil Procedure Code constitute the general procedural law on divorce. Either male or female party to a marriage in the general law can be applied for a divorce. The action shall be instituted in the district court within the local limits of jurisdiction of where either party resides or where the marriage occurred.

Initially, one spouse must start the divorce process (referred to as the "plaintiff") by meeting a known lawyer and getting advices and instructions on how to start a lawsuit to end the marriage, how to precede the case and regarding the fee structure. If the plaintiff decides to proceed further, a proxy is signed to give authority to the lawyer to represent the plaintiff in the court and to process the divorce. The plaintiff then provides every necessary details and documents that would facilitate the lawyer to file the case in the relevant court. Then the lawyer starts to write a plaint with clear discussion with the plaintiff. The plaintiff includes information on the marriage up to the separation, addresses of the parties, children of the marriage, the specific ground claimed for seeking divorce: adultery, malicious desertion or sexual impotency at the time of marriage, legal expenses and states in clear terms what the plaintiff wants. In parallel, the summons and precept to fiscal is being prepared by the lawyer: if the defendant is outside of Sri Lanka foreign summons have to be prepared. When all documents required is present, a motion is written by the lawyer asking the court to accept the documents and file with the court, serve the summons on the defendant and grant a special court date to appear in the court. After all, the lawyer subscribes the motion and the plaint.

Next the lawyer tenders the proxy, plaint documents along with one extra copies, summons, precept to fiscal, a stamped envelope addressed to defendant, AR card (Advice of delivery) and a stamp for binding chargers along with the motion to the court clerk at the record room. The clerk then inspects all documents and assigns a case number for the case, if there are no obvious errors; otherwise the lawyer is being advised to make necessary changes. Afterward, the lawyer puts the obtained case number in all documents and pays the stamp duty to the clerk who is designated for that purpose. The lawyer then hands over the documents and stamp duty receipt again to the court clerk at the record room.

When all documents required are present, the clerk enters the case number and name of the parties in the case register. Subsequently, the clerk sends all the documents to the binder to bind as a case record. After that the case file is handed over to the subject clerk who is appointed to handle divorce case documentaries. Then the clerk assigns a date and time on which the case will first be called in court. Later the case file is sent to the court register, correspondingly the court registrar checks all the material and if satisfied signs the plaint and forwards it to the judge for acceptance to issue the summons on the defendant. The judge then peruses the records and checks, if satisfied the case is accepted and orders to issue the summons on the defendant by registered post. Accordingly the subject clerk serves the summons to the defendant by registered post indicating the date and time for first court appearance, together with copy of the plaint and relevant documents which were filed by the plaintiff's lawyer. Normally after a few days of filling the case, the plaintiff's lawyer is required to meet the subject clerk to get to know about the assigned date for first court appearance and later the lawyer informs that to the client.

At the time when summons is served by registered post, the postal service requires the defendant to sign for the AR card. Accordingly, the post office has returned the card to the court, to indicate that the service was made by registered post. Once the defendant is notified for divorce, regardless of whether agrees with the plaint or not, the defendant consults with a lawyer. If the defendant wishes to proceed with a divorce, a proxy is signed to give authority to the lawyer to represent the defendant throughout the divorce process, especially by stating the number of the identity card or the passport of the defendant to certify the identity. Subsequently, the defendant's lawyer can choose either to simply appear at the summons date, serve the proxy and request a date for filing of the answer or to file an answer together with the proxy. Upon the request, a new date is assigned by the court to file the answer. Prior to filling the answer, the defendant provides every necessary details and documents that would facilitate the lawyer to prepare for the divorce. Meanwhile the lawyer writes the answer, stating either admit or deny with each numbered statement alleged in the plaint with clear discussion with the defendant. After completing the answer, the defendant must sign it and the lawyer makes two copies. Later on, the lawyer serves the plaintiff's lawyer with a copy of the answer by mail. Next, takes the original answer to the court on the assigned date to fill an answer. At that time, the lawyer has to state either the defendant is contesting or not contesting the divorce.

When the defendant makes no defense: not contesting the divorce, the court proceeds to hear the case ex parte forthwith. Usually, the plaintiff' lawyer gets the opportunity to ask questions from the plaintiff in order to place evidence before the court in support of pleadings. If the court satisfied that the plaintiff is entitled to get the divorce, enters such judgment in favors of the plaintiff and enter decree accordingly. The court serves a copy of the decree entered on the defendant in the manner prescribed for the service of summons. When the defendant is contesting the divorce, the court fixes the day of hearing. Correspondingly, fifteen days before the date fixed for hearing, each party files a list of witnesses to be called at the hearing and a list of the documents relied upon and to be produced at the hearing and gives a copy of everything that to the other side. If either party does not file the witness list, the court may sanction you by not allowing you to call your witnesses. Meanwhile each party tries to best prepare their witnesses. On the day fixed for hearing of the action, at first both sides present their issues to be solved and the court shall deal with the stated issues only. After that, the plaintiff's lawyer gets the opportunity to ask questions from the plaintiff in order to place evidence before the court in support of pleadings, called direct examination. Then the other side can cross-examine the plaintiff. The plaintiff's lawyer can then ask more questions called re-direct, to try to fix any inaccurate information that arose from the cross-examination. The plaintiff's lawyer has the opportunity to ask the witnesses' questions and repeats this cycle until all witnesses for their side are done. The defendant's lawyer goes next and repeats the cycle described above. Such proceedings are usually lengthy. The court may from time to time adjourn the hearing of the action.

Finally, the judge issues a decision after considering all the issues presented at hearing. The judge's decision may be pronounced in open court, either at once or on some future day. Within fourteen days of the service of the decree, either party liable to appeal against the decree to the Court of Appeal. The grounds for appeal usually allege that the district judge made an error either in procedure or in interpreting the law. for the system.

# 4

# Theoretical Background

In this chapter, the background and the foundation of proposed framework for legal service collaboration modeling have been briefed. It starts by introducing the related projects available for legal solution development and collaboration modeling. Then the widely accepted standards from the UN/CEFACT for electronic business process modeling have been briefly introduced as it was selected as the basis of our proposal discussed in the Chapter 5. Finally, BPMN was explained in brief as it has been used for specification and documentation of proposed transaction patterns and collaborations.

## 4.1 Related Projects in Legal Solution Development

- JWeB

  The JWeB project [5], funded by the European Commission in IST Program, has the objective to implement a secure, web based Judicial Collaboration Platform (JCP) supporting cross-border investigations on criminal matters through the integration of Computer Supported Cooperative Work (CSCW), secure information exchange, videoconference and advanced knowledge management. However these contributions are at very lower technical level and not addressed much on higher level legal service collaboration modeling like in our work.

- SecurE-Justice

  The SecurE-Justice project [6] aims at introducing an advanced information management system in the field of justice to manage three main phases; investigation, criminal action and debate. Chiefly, the SecurE-Justice system provides a common platform to manage all these phases using a unique collaboration framework and an innovative technological solution to integrate and define a workflow model to facilitate the continuous collaboration of the investigation authorities and the judging magistrate within a secure and private working environment. Anyhow, these contributions are also not directly related and addressed legal service collaboration modeling as of interest in our work.

## 4.2 UN/CEFACT's Collaboration Modeling

For electronic business collaboration modeling there are huge collections of approaches, some are with proprietary limited industry/developer participation and some are globally accepted open standards with wider industry/developer participation. However, among globally accepted open standards, UN/CEFACT's Modeling Methodology (UMM) [8] is well known and adopted in many different industries.

Techniques and Methodologies Working Group (TMWG) of UN/CEFACT proposes UMM to model business processes and to support the development of existing and "The Next Generation" of Electronic Data Interchange (EDI) for e-businesses. The main objective of UMM is to capture common business practices into standardized business models. This will enable small and medium sized companies to engage in emerging e-business practices in a protocol neutral and future proof manner independent of proprietary technologies. The primary scope of UMM is to provide a perspective of business transactions limited to those aspects regarding the making of business decisions and commitments among persons, which are needed for the description of a business transaction. The UMM provides a procedure for specifying collaborative business processes involving information exchanges. One of the completed projects within UN/CEFACT is ebXML Project [4] that contributed with a complete XML based suite electronic message exchange targeting general business applications. Although these recommendations and XML based contributions are targeted towards generic business applications, it was evident that there is no complete universal work similar to UN/CEFACT's recommendations for e-business designing to be adopted in the legal sector.

UMM meta-model facilitates the specification of reusable, reproducible process models that are technology and protocol insensitive and advices well defined workflow for electronic business collaboration designs. Mainly, UMM meta-models consist of four views in order to describe different business concerns during collaboration designing, so that each business process and information model can be viewed from a number of perspectives. These are Business Operations Map (BOM) meta-model, Business Requirements View (BRV) meta-model, Business Transaction View (BTV) meta-model and Business Service View (BSV) meta-model [8].

- BOM meta-model - partitioning of business processes into business areas and business categories

- BRV meta-model - specification view of a business process model that captures the use case scenarios, inputs, outputs, constraints and system boundaries for business transactions and their interrelationships

- BTV meta-model - view of a business process model that captures the semantics of business information entities and their flow of exchange between roles as they perform business activities

- BSV meta-model - view of a business process model that specifies the network component services and agents and their information exchange as interactions necessary to execute and validate a business process

These perspectives support an incremental model construction methodology and provide levels of specification granularity that are suitable for communicating the model to business domain experts, business application integrators and network application solution providers.

Although the UMM meta-model consist of four views in order to describe different business concerns during collaboration designing, our work mainly focused on to the Business Transaction View (BTV), as it defines the orchestration of the business collaboration and structures the business information exchanged among trading parties.

## 4.2.1   Business Transaction View

BTV has been mainly developed for business domain for information exchange between buyers and sellers for business activities. In UMM, a business collaboration protocol is specified as a flow of business transaction activities. A Business Transaction is a unit of work though which business parties exchange business information and signals between them. These business information and signals are in agreement in format, sequence and time interval and etc. These information and signals are exchanged between buyers and sellers. This exchange is called Actions in the business domain. These Business Actions consist of two parts. Requesting Business Activities and Responding Business Activities. The activities are performed by an actor. An actor is requesting a Business Service (BS) and it is called a Requesting Business Activity. While a response to such request is called Responding Business Activity. When a transaction completes, all the interactions within it succeed or it is rolled back. Furthermore, the flow between different Business Transactions can be choreographed through Business Collaboration Protocols. The choreography is best suited to define the commitment between the partners. Nevertheless, each partner is responsible to implement system that is complaint to the agreed choreography. Business Collaboration Protocols should be used in cases where transaction rollback is inappropriate.

The BTV is a specification of a business transaction according to six predefined, legally binding patterns. Generally, UMM includes such six predefined, legally binding patterns to model business transaction activities and their associated service collaborations.

**UMM Transaction Patterns**

Patterns are reusable, generalized business process abstractions that can be applied to many domains. A meta-model provides the syntax and grammar for expressing designs. Patterns are subjective constructions that meet the requirements of specific business process scenarios. Patterns are applications of the meta-model to common business process and information representations. Common business process and information representations capture common structure and semantics applicable to specific business process domains. The key to repeatable business process and information model constructions is the application of patterns to specific business process scenarios. While patterns can be expressed for business processes at various levels, the UMM currently includes patterns for business transaction activities and their associated service collaborations. The business transaction patterns are:

1.      Commercial Transaction Pattern
2.      Query/Response Transaction Pattern
3.      Request/Response Transaction Pattern
4.      Request/Confirm Transaction Pattern
5.      Information Distribution Transaction Pattern
6.      Notification Transaction Pattern

These business transaction activity patterns comprehensively cover all the known legally binding collaborations at the lowest level of Request/Response interaction between two business applications. Accordingly, this set of original transaction patterns is selected as the basis for our proposed universal framework. In order to develop the proposed collaboration modeling framework, we have analyzed and extended these transaction patterns based on the legal sector requirement we were explored during our analysis.

**Commercial Transaction Pattern**

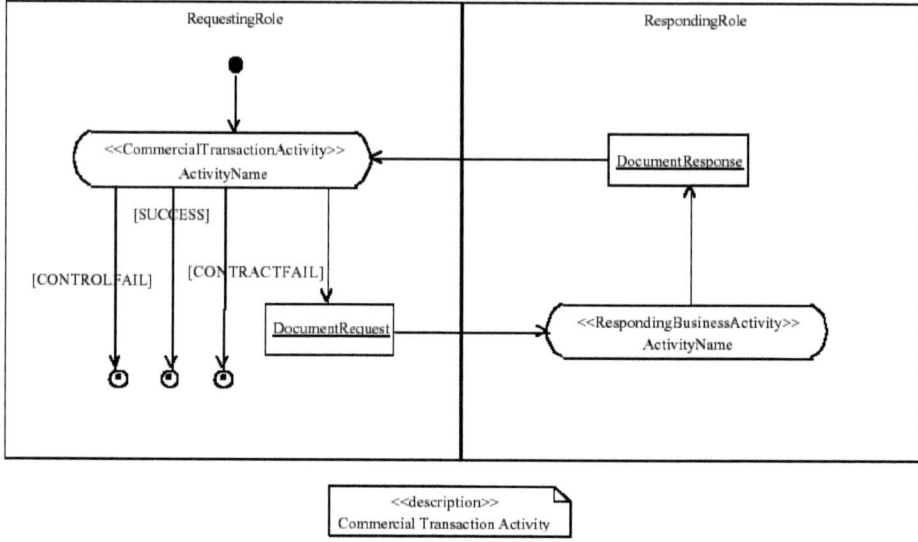

Figure 4.1: Commercial Transaction Pattern

This design pattern is best used to model the 'offer and acceptance' Business transaction process that results in a residual obligation between both parties to fulfil the terms of the contract. The pattern specifies an originating business activity sending a business document to a responding business activity that may return a business signal or business document as the last responding message.

**Query/Response Transaction Pattern**

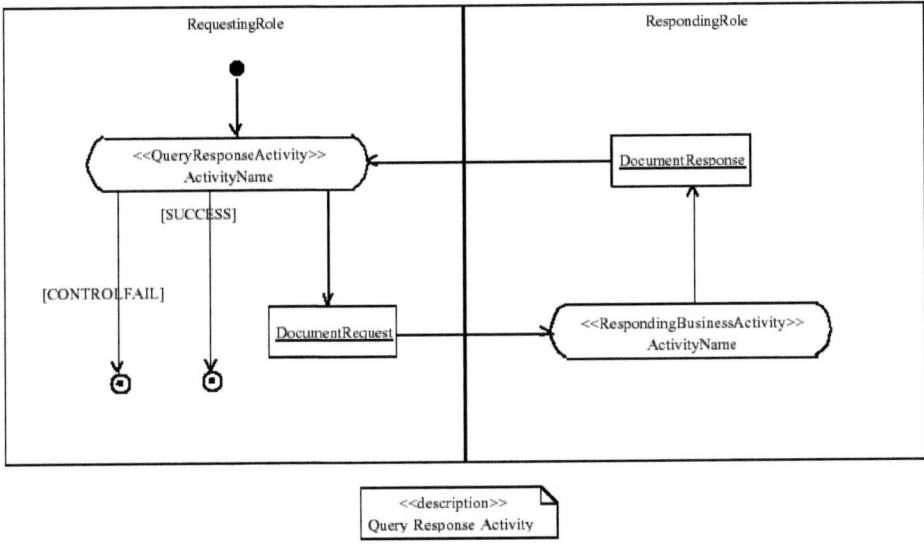

Figure 4.2: Query/Response Transaction Pattern

The Query/Response design pattern specifies a query for information that a responding partner already has e.g. against fixed data set that resides in a database. The response comprises zero or more results each of which meets the constraining criterion in the query.

**Request/Response Transaction Pattern**

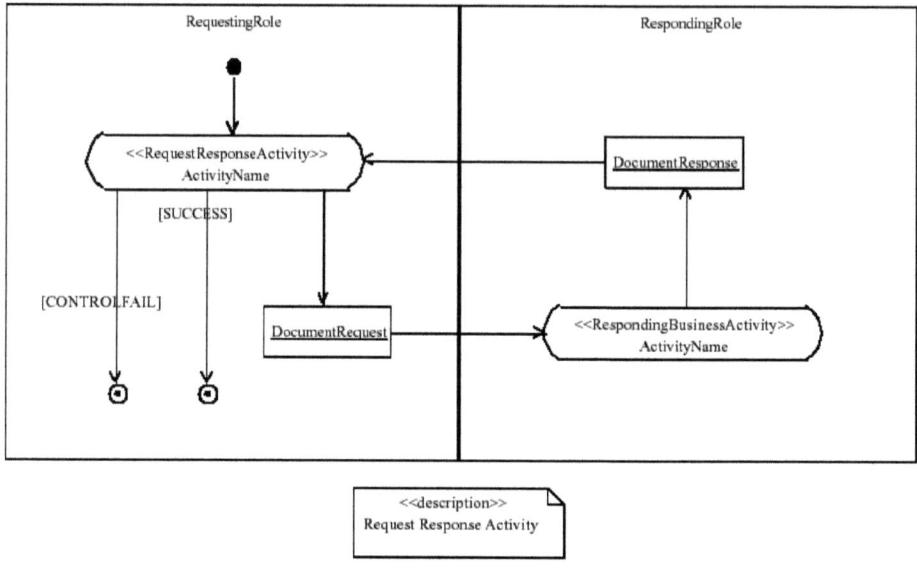

Figure 4.3: Request/Response Transaction Pattern

The Request/Response activity pattern shall be used for business contracts when an initiating partner requests information that a responding partner already has and when the request for business information requires a complex interdependent set of results.

**Request/Confirm Transaction Pattern**

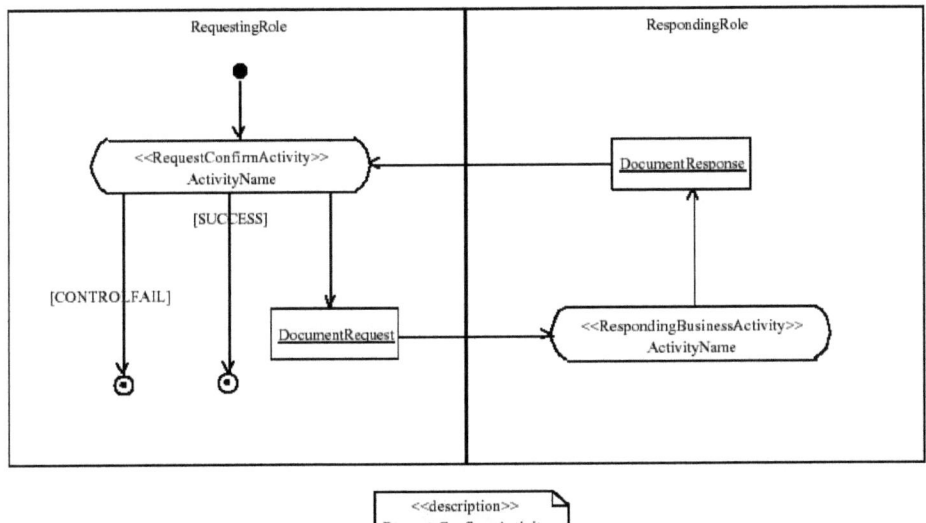

Figure 4.4: Request/Confirm Transaction Pattern

The Request/Confirm activity pattern shall be used for business contracts when an initiating partner requests confirmation about their status with respect to previously established contracts or with respect to a responding partner's business rules.

**Notification Transaction Pattern**

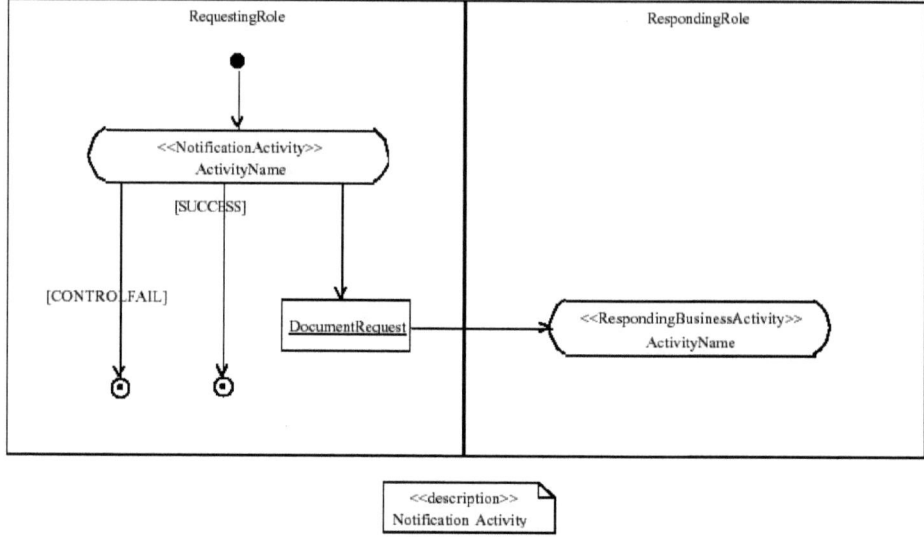

Figure 4.5: Request/Notification Transaction Pattern

This pattern specifies the exchange of a notifying business document and the return of an acknowledgement of receipt business signal. This pattern is used to model a formal information exchange business transaction that therefore has non-repudiation requirements.

**Information Distribution Transaction Pattern**

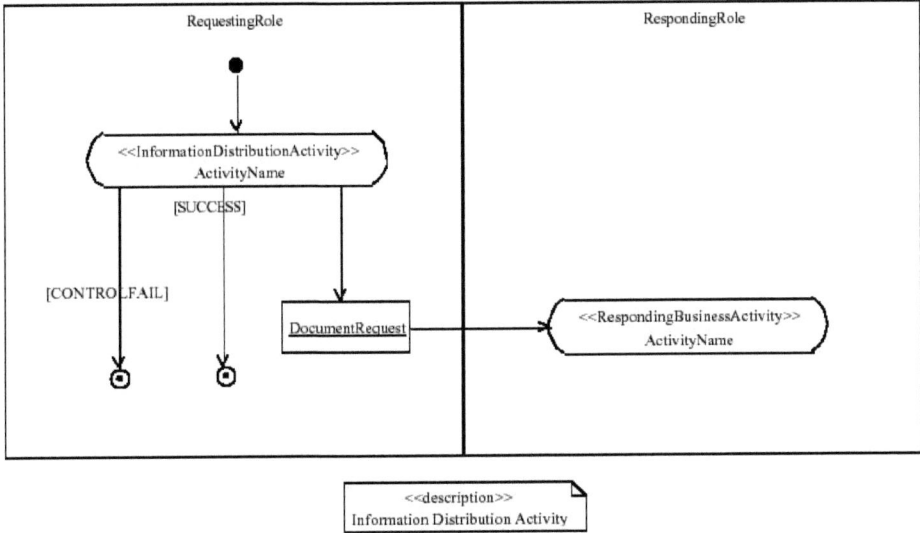

Figure 4.6: Request/Information Distribution Transaction Pattern

This pattern specifies the exchange of a requesting business document and the return of an acknowledgement of receipt signal. The pattern is used to model an informal information exchange business transaction that therefore has no nonrepudiation requirements.

## 4.3 Business Process Modeling Notation

Business Process Modeling Notation (BPMN) [3] is an open standard developed by Business Process Management Initiative (BPMI) [2]. The goal of BPMN is to provide a rich set of readily comprehensible notation for a wide spectrum of stakeholders from business domain experts to technical developers. The ambition of the BPMN project is to bridge the gap between business process design and their technical realizations. Especially, BPMN provides businesses with the capability of understanding their internal business procedures in a graphical notation and gives organizations the ability to communicate these procedures in a standard manner. Furthermore, the graphical notation facilitates the understanding of the performance collaborations and business transactions between the organizations.

There are three different process categories that BPMN could assist modeling and specification. Firstly, Internal/Private Process that limits it's all activities to a particular business party or particular organization. Secondly, Interface/Public Processes that describes only all activities that lead to communication with external parties. Thirdly, Global/Collaboration Processes that show how two more interface processes are inter-connected in their collaborations. The BPMN specification provides a graphical notation for expressing business processes in a Business Process Diagram (BPD). The objective of BPMN is to support business process management by both technical users and business users by providing a notation that is intuitive to business users yet able to represent complex process semantics. The BPMN specification also provides a mapping between the graphics of the notation to the underlying constructs of execution languages.

In the literature, there are process specification notations ranging from lower level scripting languages to human readable visual notations, using symbolic expressions. However two main requirements have been identified in relation to our research work. First requirement is the need for increased readability by non-technical users, who may participate in collaboration modeling tasks. Second requirement is need for easy mapping mechanism to transform these visual models into lower technical level implementations. In the context, BPMN fits very nicely with our requirements.

### 4.3.1   Type of Business Processes

A variety of information is being communicated to a wide range of stakeholders in the business process modeling tasks in business domain. Consequently, BPMN is intended to serve as common language to bridge the communication gap that frequently occurs between business process design and implementation. In order to serve this purpose, business processes can be defined at three different levels of sub processes: Private Business Process, Public Business Process and Global Business Process.

- Private (Internal) Business Processes - business processes that are internal to a specific organization

- Abstract (Public) Business Processes - business processes that model interaction between private processes and other processes or participants. These processes consist only of activities that are used to communicate outside private business processes.

- Collaboration (Global) Business Processes - these processes model the interaction between two or more business parties. The internal activities of the private business processes are detailed in addition to the message exchanges between them. These interactions are defined as a sequence of activities that represent the exchange message between the entities involved. A single collaboration process may be mapped to various collaboration languages. However, basic type of sub-model within an end-to-end BPMN that we are interested in and relevant for our work is collaboration processes as we are to develop framework that facilitate legal service collaboration modeling. Therefore all BPMN syntactic representations that we are to introduce in proceeding sections belong to this group.

### 4.3.2   Business Process Modeling Notation Core Elements

The diagrams that visualize BPMN process specifications are called Business Process Diagrams (BPD) [3]. The BPD is a graphical representation of a business process flow, which consists of a sequence of activity elements and flow controls elements. BPD can be constructed by combining different graphical objects according to rules that have been defined under BPMN Specification Releases. Again these graphical objects can be categorized into sub-groups as listed below.

- Primary modeling elements - There are three primary modeling elements in BPMN as Events, Activities and Gateways.

- Elements to connect primary modeling elements - There are three elements that can be used to connect primary modeling elements as Sequence Flow, Message Flow and Association.

- Elements to group primary modeling elements - There are two elements that can be used to group primary modeling elements as Pools and Lanes.

Below section borrowed from BPMN specification release lists different notations that have been proposed to symbolize BPD core elements. This is not the complete set of core elements that can be found in original specification; instead it is a selected sub-set for our work.

- Event - An event is something that "happens" during the course of a business process. These events affect the flow of the process and usually have a cause (trigger) or an impact (result).

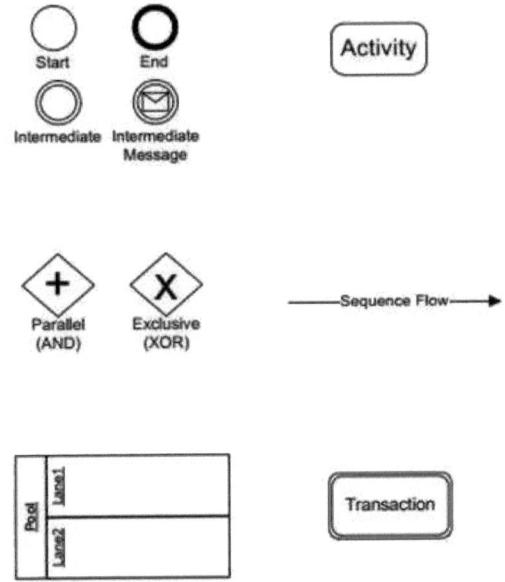

Figure 4.7: BPMN Notations

There are three types of Events, based on when they affect the flow: Start, Intermediate, and End.

- Activity - An activity is a generic term for work that company performs. An activity can be atomic or non-atomic (compound). The types of activities that are a part of a Process Model are: Process, Sub-Process, and Task. Tasks and Sub-Processes are rounded rectangles. Processes are either unbounded or a contained within a Pool.

- Gateway - A Gateway is used to control the divergence and convergence of Sequence Flow. Thus, it will determine branching, forking, merging, and joining of paths. Internal Markers will indicate the type of behavior control.

- Sequence Flow - A Sequence Flow is used to show the order that activities will be performed in a Process.

- Pool - A Pool represents a Participant in a Process. It is also acts as a "swimlane" and a graphical container for partitioning a set of activities from other Pools, usually in the context of B2B situations.

- Lane - A Lane is a sub-partition within a Pool and will extend the entire length of the Pool, either vertically or horizontally. Lanes are used to organize and categorize activities.

- Transaction - A transaction is a Sub-Process that is supported by special protocol that insures that all parties involved have complete agreement that the activity should be completed or cancelled. The attributes of the activity will determine if the activity is a transaction (double-lined rectangle).

# 5

# Legal Collaboration Modeling Framework (LCMF)

In the following chapter, a set of primitive transaction patterns to model legal service collaborations are suggested, according to the domain requirement described in Chapter 3.

As introduced at the very beginning, when attempting to develop ICT solutions for formalizing highly dynamic and complex information exchanges among many different legal sector participants, modeling complex multi-party collaboration workflows have been resulted challenging for solution developers. One straight forward approach to address these complexity issues in multi-party collaboration modeling is to break them down into more manageable binary collaborations. In the proposed framework, we have developed a set of primitive transaction patterns in compliance with but by extending the original transaction patterns that has been proposed in UN/CEFACT's recommendations. However, during our investigation in legal domain, we have experienced and realized significant differences between generic business trading procedures compared against to legal service collaborations. These differences resulted limitations on adopting the original UN/CEFACT's proposals as it is. However in this work, extensions have been proposed to UMM with the objective of accommodating demanding legal sector requirements while ensuring the alignment with UN/CEFACT's recommendations. Consequently, we have identified several different transaction patterns to model binary legal collaborations as listed below.

- Multilateral Offer and Acceptance

- Query/Response

  - Information Querying
  - Examine/Testify
    * DirectExamine Witness of Plaintiff/Testify
    * IndirectExamine Witness of Plaintiff /Testify
    * Re-directExamine Witness of Plaintiff /Testify
    * DirectExamine Witness of Defendant/Testify
    * IndirectExamine Witness of Defendant /Testify
    * Re-directExamine Witness of Defendant /Testify

- Request/Response

  - Request Court's Response
  - Request Plaintiff's Response
  - Request Defendant's Response
  - Request Witness's Response

- Request Case Hearing Status/Confirmation
- Request Made at Court
  - Request/Order
  - Request/Grant
- Order Completion
  - Order Plaintiff/Completion
  - Order Defendant/Completion
  - Order Court Personnel/Completion
- Case Hearing Information Notification
  - Direct Notification
    * State Plaintiff's Issues
    * State Defendant's Issues
    * Judgment Notification
  - Indirect Notification

Our initial intuition is that using these primitive transaction patterns, highly dynamic and complex legal service collaborations could easily be modeled. In order to background of our intuition and semantic representations attempted to capture has been summarized in the following sub-sections. Furthermore we have utilized BPMN notation to construct proposed transaction patterns and also this specific pattern formation is inspired by the transaction patterns contribution in UN/CEFACT's recommendations . Mainly activity, event and gateway placement in BPMN lanes of business process diagrams represent requesting and responding roles of the legal system and completion of activities resulting events with global interest.

## 5.1 Transaction Patterns

### 5.1.1 Multilateral Offer and Acceptance Transaction Pattern

This specialized transaction pattern could be considered as an extension to original UMM Commercial Transaction Pattern. The requirement for adaption of this pattern is to establish a contract for governing collaboration with legal domain roles. In this situation, multilateral parties may enter into an agreement with obligations to take part in legal case proceedings.

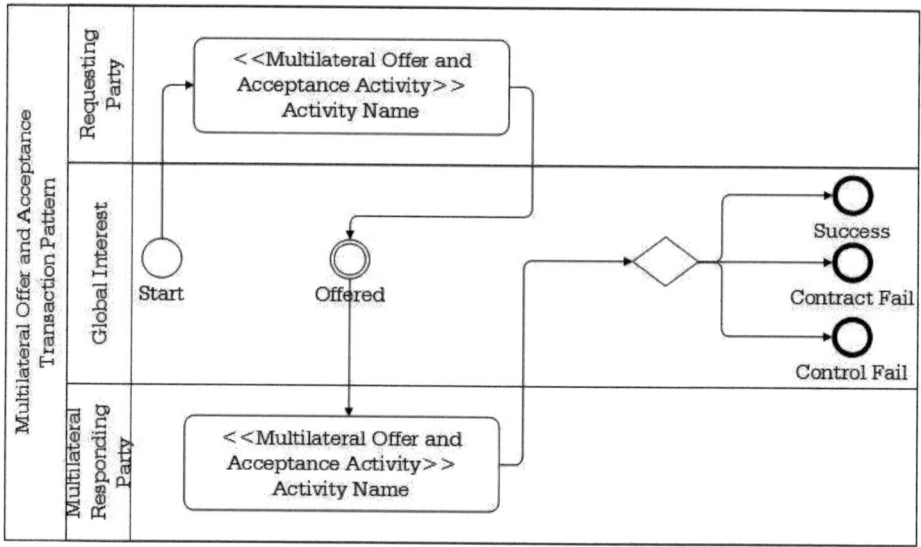

Figure 5.1: Multilateral and Offer Acceptance Transaction Pattern

As in the above diagram, this pattern has three possible outcomes. The success event is named as "Success" where multilateral parties get into an agreement. There could also be a possibility of "Contract Fail" event where either party rejects an offer. Finally, the "Control Fail" event, means due to some technical issues, either party is unable to collaborate with each other to get into an agreement.

## 5.1.2 Query/Response Transaction Patterns

There is a transaction pattern called Query/Response in original UMM recommendations that demands to request information that responding party already has. During our investigation in legal sector, we get explored the need for need for specialization of Query/Response transaction into two.

One is named as Information Querying, which is very much identical to original Que-ry/Response transaction pattern. The requirement for adaptation of this transaction pattern is querying the content that the responder already has. For an instance court clerk, Mr. Tennakoon requests names and addresses of all witnesses in a divorce hearing from court's record room, could be given as an example.

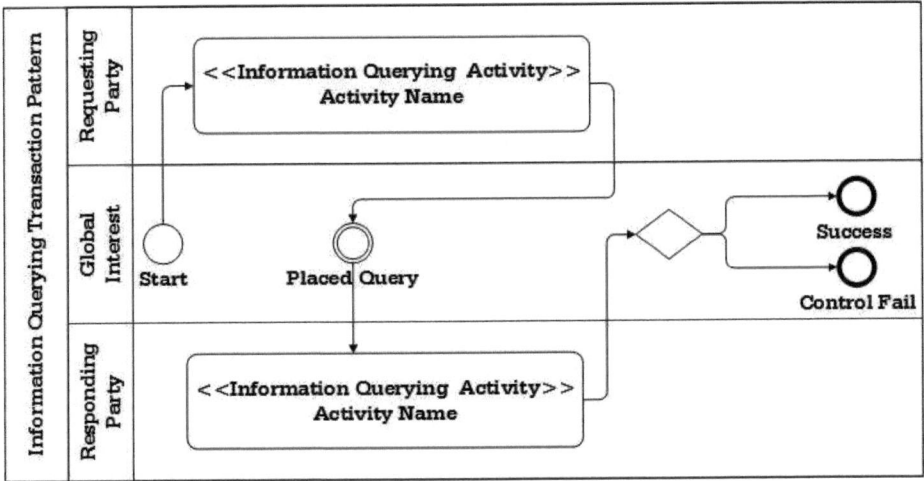

Figure 5.2: Information Querying Transaction Pattern

The other transaction pattern that we have developed is called Examine/Testify. The requirement for adaptation of this transaction pattern is examining for information that the responding party already knows. Although this could be considered as an extension to original UMM Query/Response transaction pattern, we have further specialized this pattern into three sub types according to sector requirements that we were explored during our analysis. Therefore the first sub-type of Examine/Testify transaction pattern is named as DirectExamine/Testify through which a lawyer asks questions from the responder (client) in order to place evidence before the court in support of pleadings. The second sub-type of Examine/Testify transaction pattern is named as IndirectExamine/Testify through which the other side cross-examines the responder. The third sub-type of Examine/Testify transaction pattern is named as Re-directExamine/Testify through which the lawyer asks more questions from the responder to fix any inaccurate information. In the first place, the plaintiff's lawyer gets the opportunity to perform these three transaction patterns sequentially until all witnesses for their side are done and generally the defendant's lawyer goes next. Accordingly, we have further specialized these transaction patterns as DirectExamine Witness of Plaintiff/Testify, IndirectExamine Witness of Plaintiff /Testify, Re-directExamine Witness of Plaintiff /Testify, DirectExamine Witness of Defendant/Testify, IndirectExamine Witness of Defendant /Testify and Re-directExamine Witness of Defendant /Testify. In these situations, each responder is obliged to place requested information before the court.

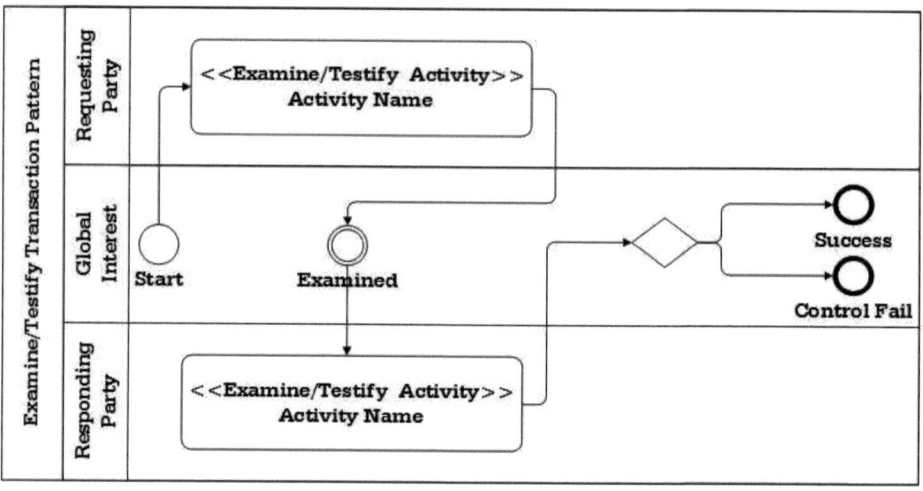

Figure 5.3: Basic Semantics of Examine/Testify Transaction Patterns

However, syntactic BPMN representation of these transaction patterns kept identical. It is important to notice in these Query/Response transaction patterns that the final results always evaluates to a success. This is because of query always returned zero or more results. The other possible outcome is "Control Fail" event means due to some technical error, requestor is not receiving intended outcome of the transaction.

### 5.1.3 Request/Response Transaction Patterns

There is a transaction pattern called Request/Response in original UMM recommendations that demands complex calculation to provide requested information to the recipient. In analogous to this transaction pattern, there is a need where requested information that is not readily available but needs complex elicitation process to be executed in responding party's end. However, during our investigation in legal sector, we get explored the need for specialization of Request/Response transaction into four sub categories that might carry different weight-ages and necessity for differentiation in case hearing procedures. These patterns are named as Request Court's Response, Request Plaintiff's Response, Request Defendant's Response and Request Witness's Response. A specific example instantiated from Request Plaintiff's Response transaction patterns is court requests for certified copies of police reports from a plaintiff, Mr. Perera in a divorce case. Such documents may not readily be available with him but needs to follow the complex procedure to get certified copies of original police reports from authorized parties.

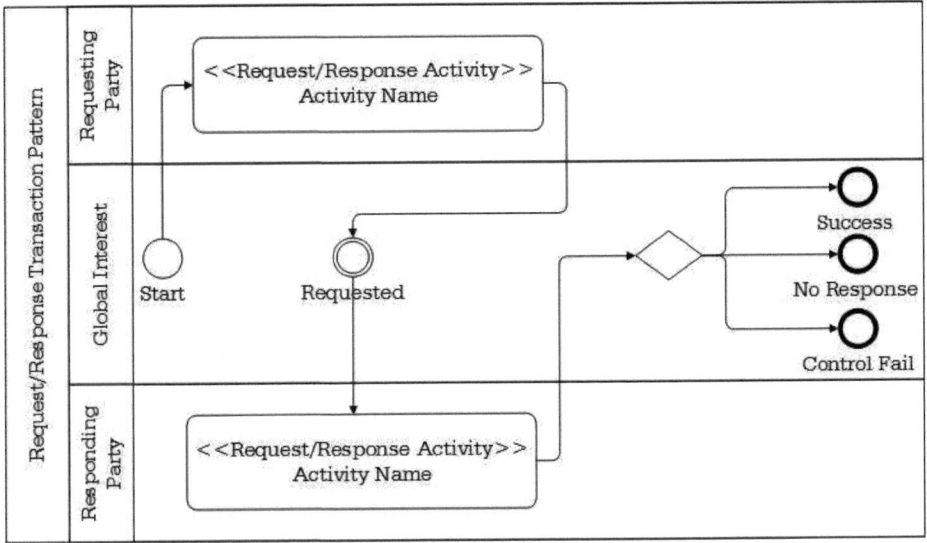

Figure 5.4: Basic Semantics of Request/Response Transaction Patterns

In general, the requirement for adaptation of Request/Response transaction patterns is requesting for information that the responding partner not readily has or available in connected information-base but needs complex elicitation process to be executed in responding party's end to provide the requested information. Similar to the above transaction patterns, even here there are two common possible outcomes as "Success" event, where responder able to provide requested information and "Control Fail" event where due to some technical error, requestor is not receiving intended information of the transaction. There could also be a possibility of "No Response" event where responder neglects or deny provisioning requested information.

### 5.1.4 Request Case Hearing Status/Confirmation Transaction Pattern

There is a transaction pattern called Request/Confirm in original UMM recommendations that demands the status of an existing agreement. Request Case Hearing Status/Confirmation is much identical to this original transaction pattern. The requirement for adaptation of Request Case Status Hearing Confirmation pattern is requesting confirmation about status with respect to started case hearing proceedings. In this situation, responder is obliged to provide requested status information.

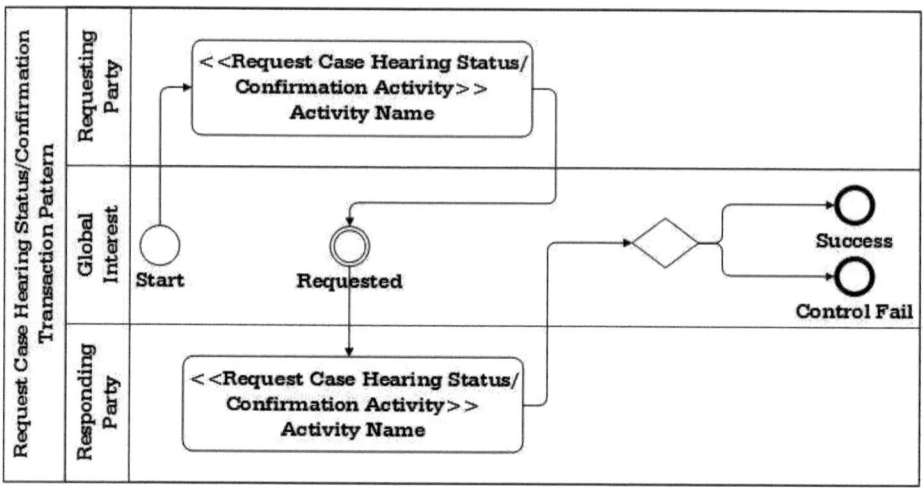

Figure 5.5: Request Case Hearing Status/Confirmation Transaction Pattern

The only two possible outcomes of this pattern are "Success" and "Control Fail". As responder is obliged to provide a response this pattern always evaluates to a "Success", if not a technical issue. A specific example instantiated from this pattern is a plaintiff, Mr. Perera in divorce case requests status information about the filled case from the court.

subsectionRequest Made at Court Transaction Patterns

Request Made at Court Transaction Patterns are very special patterns that are not common in generic business collaborations. During our investigation in legal domain, we get explored the need for further specify the requests made at a court by either party to a case into two.

One is named as Request/Order through which a lawyer requests to the court to make an order. If the court is satisfied with the request, then court shall set an order. If the defendant in a divorce case, Mr. Ekanayake fails to appear at the summons date, then the plaintiff's lawyer, Mr. Perera requests the court to order for serve summons personally on the defendant by delivering through the fiscal, which would be an instance of the Request/Order pattern.

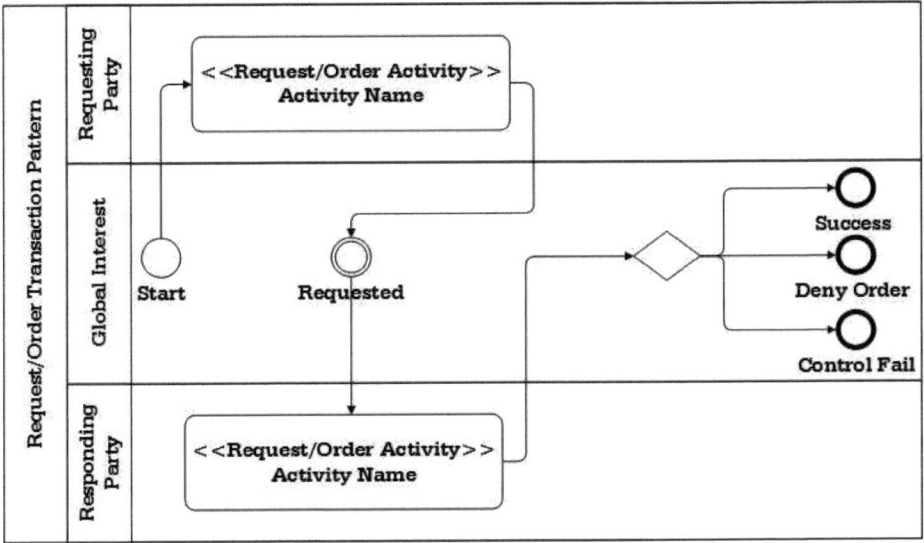

Figure 5.6: Request/Order Transaction Pattern

As in the above diagram, this pattern has three possible outcomes. The success event is named as "Success" where the court sets an order. There could also be a possibility of "Deny Order" event where the court denies provisioning the requested order. The other possible outcome is "Control Fail" event.

The other specialization is Request/Grant pattern. Through this pattern, either party to a case could request to the court to concede for conduct a specific legal proceeding. If the court is satisfied, then court shall grant the request. If the defendant in a divorce case, Mr. Ekanayake fails to appear on the day fixed, then the plaintiff's lawyer, Mr. Perera requests the court to hear the case ex parte forthwith, which would be an instance of the Request/Grant pattern. Even here, there are two possible outcomes as in most of the transaction patterns. Besides them, due to not having sufficient reasoning to grant the request, there is another possible outcome called "Deny Grant" event where the court denies provisioning the granting of request.

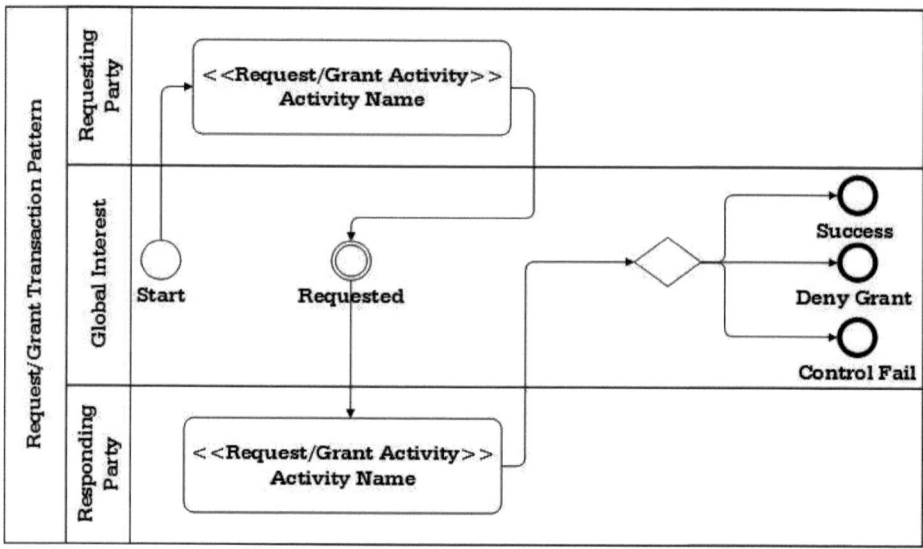

Figure 5.7: Request/Grant Transaction Pattern

### 5.1.5 Order/Completion Transaction Patterns

Order/Completion transaction patterns are also very special patterns that are not complying with the original transaction patterns that have been proposed in UN/CEFACT's recommendations. The requirement for adaptation of this transaction patterns are ordering a specific legal proceeding with respect to on-going case hearing. In this situation, the person who has received the order is obliged to fulfill it. During our investigation in legal sector, we get explored the need for specialization of Order/Completion transaction further into three sub categories that might carry different weight-ages, as Order Plaintiff/Completion, Order Defendant/Completion, and Order Court Personnel/Completion.

Generally, the only two possible outcomes of this pattern are "Success" and "Control Fail". As receiver is obliged to fulfill the order this pattern always evaluates to a "Success" if not a technical issue. A specific example instantiated from this pattern is court orders to file a list of witnesses to be called at the hearing and a list of the documents relied upon and to be produced at the hearing before the date fixed for hearing. In this situation, each party to the case is obliged to fulfill the order.

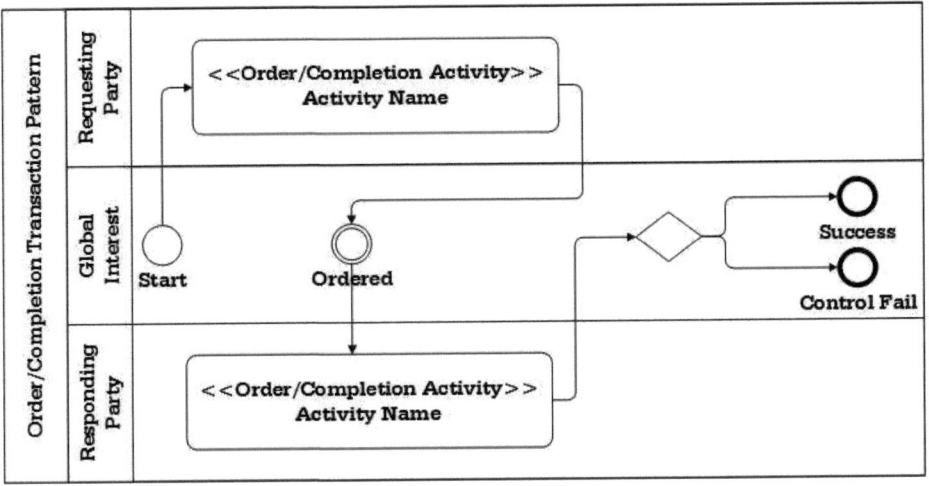

Figure 5.8: Basic Semantics of Order/Completion Transaction Patterns

### 5.1.6 Case Hearing Information Notification Transaction Patterns

There is an original UMM transaction pattern called, Notification transaction pattern that can be used to notify recipient with non-repudiation requirement. However, during our investigation in legal sector, we get explored the need for further specify the Notification transaction into two. Both these transaction patterns are very much identical to each other. The only difference is the final intended party of the notification.

One is named as Direct Notification through which intended recipient is directly informed with some notice. When the defendant, Mr. Bandara is contesting the divorce, court fixes a day of hearing and pronounces it in open court, which would be an instance of the Direct Notification transaction pattern. In the meantime, we get noticed the need for specializations of Direct Notification pattern, called State Issues transaction pattern which could be performed by either party to a case and Judgment Notification transaction pattern.

The other specialization of Case Hearing Information Notification transaction pattern is to notify immediate recipient with the intension of communicating to intended party of the notice. When court adjourns the hearing of the action, both parties in the divorce case are notified about the next assigned date with the intension of informing that to their witnesses, which would be an instance of the Indirect Notification transaction pattern. Both these transaction patterns are very much identical to each other. The only difference is the final intended party of the notification.

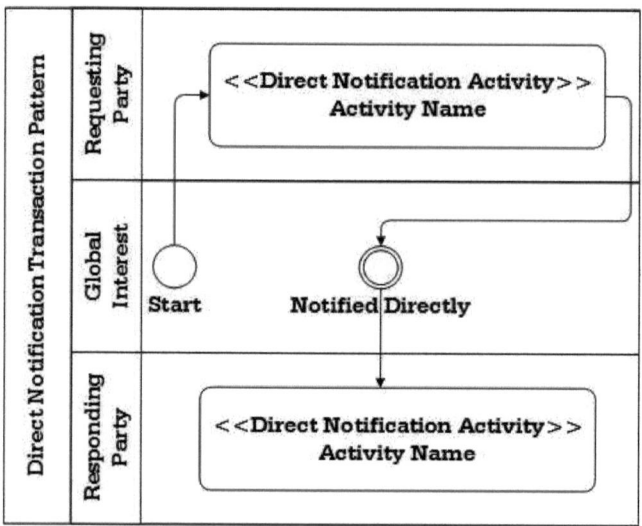

Figure 5.9: Basic Semantics of Direct Notification Transaction Patterns

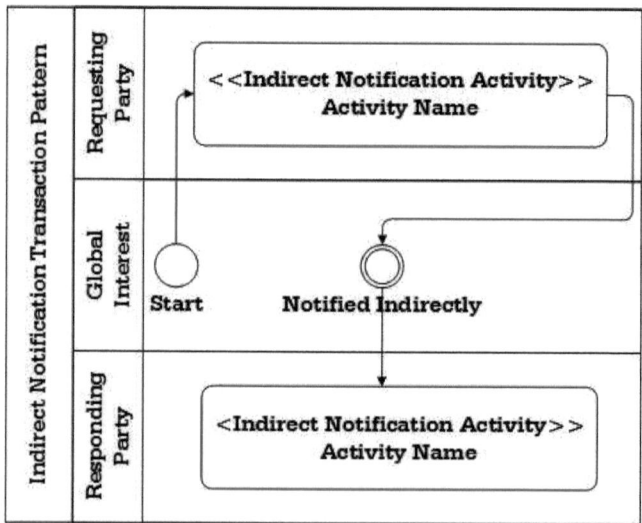

Figure 5.10: Indirect Notification Transaction Pattern

Furthermore, during our analysis, we have noticed that the distribution of information without non-repudiation requirements is not lawful throughout the sector. Especially, since there is an original UMM transaction pattern called Information Distribution to notify recipient without enforcing non-repudiation requirement, it makes clear that such pattern is hard to adopt for legal domain application development.

# 6

# Application and Evaluation of Legal Collaboration Modeling Framework

Although the main objective of this research work is to introduce a modeling framework with the intention of facilitating legal service collaboration modeling, in this chapter, we have very briefly illustrated two of the most prominent applications of the proposed transaction patterns in legal service collaboration designing process following with superficial theoretical evaluation that we completed against the legal sector experts to ensure that the proposed patterns are sufficient for modeling legal collaborations.

## 6.1 Application of Legal Collaboration Modeling Framework

The proposed transaction patterns can be used as basic building blocks in the process of constructing complex multi-party legal service collaboration models. Intuitive illustrations of such applications are given below.

### 6.1.1 Case Filling Procedure

There, we have utilized three of the primitive transactions patterns introduced above for the development of collaboration model for Case Filling process.

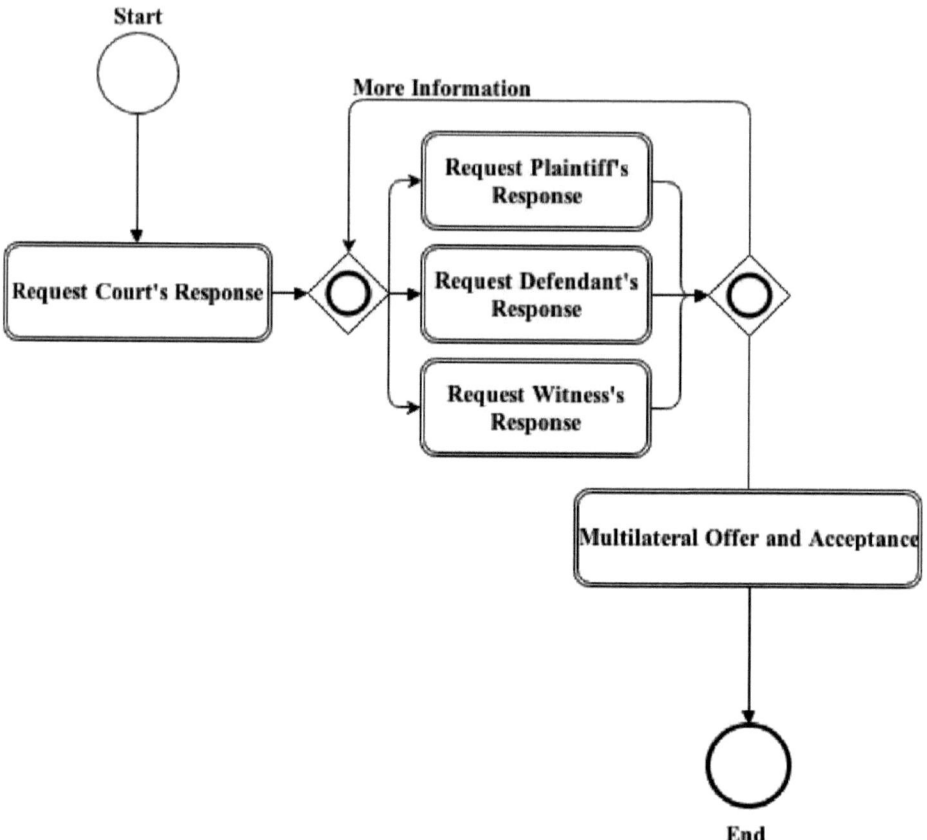

Figure 6.1: Collaboration Diagram for Case Filling Procedure

As shown in figure, this collaborating situation could be considered as proceeding via three main phases; Filing Request, Information Gathering and Contract Establishment. During the Filing Request phase, a request to the court is made from a party of a legal case for enacting the case filling process via Request Court's Response transaction. When the court receives the request, enters into next phase, Information Gathering. During this phase, every necessary details and documents related to the contract to be established are gathered from each party to the case via Request Plaintiff's Response, Request Defendant's Response and Request Witness's Response transactions. There, any possible combinations of requesting the responses are allowed. Finally, during the Contract Establishment phase, both parties to the case get into a legally bound obligation as the court is satisfied with the gathered information to process with the case. With generating the pre-requisite for enact hearing, the case filing process terminates.

### 6.1.2   Courts Hearing Procedure

There, we have utilized four primitive transactions patterns introduced above for develop collaboration model for district court case hearing legal proceeding.

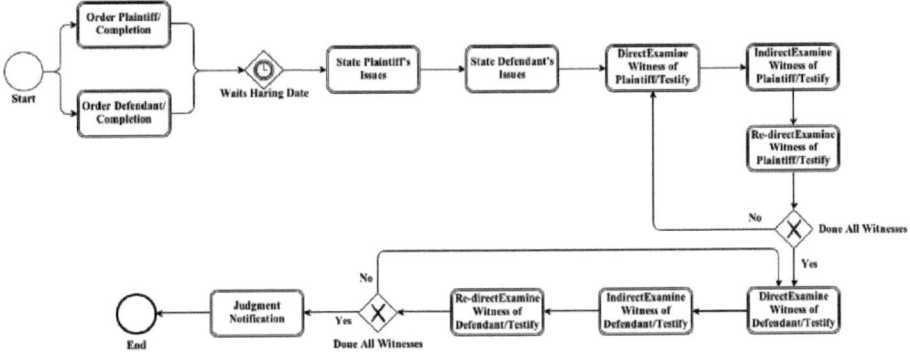

Figure 6.2: Collaboration diagram for Courts Hearing Procedure

As in the above illustration, case hearing situation could be considered as proceeding via four main collaborating phases; Fling Lists, State Issues, Examination and Judgment. During Filing Lists phase court orders each party to an action for filing a list of witnesses to be called and a list of the documents relied upon at the case hearing before the date fixed for hearing of the action via Order/Completion transaction. On the case hearing day, State Issues phase executes, where both parties present their issues to be solved before the court via State Plaintiff's Issues and State Defendant's Issues transactions. After that, during Examination phase the plaintiff's lawyer gets the opportunity to ask questions from their witness in order to place evidence before the court in support of pleadings via DirectExamine/Testify transaction. Then the other side cross-examines the witness via IndirectExamine/Testify transaction. The plaintiff's lawyer then asks more questions via Re-directExamine/Testify transaction to fix any inaccurate information that arose from the cross-examination. The plaintiff's lawyer has repeats this cycle until all witnesses for their side are done. The defendant's lawyer goes next and repeats the cycle. Finally, during Judgment phase the judge issues a decision after considering all the issues presented at hearing. With pronouncing the decision in open court, case hearing process terminates.

## 6.2   Evaluation of Legal Collaboration Modeling Framework

A variety of proposed legal service transaction patterns could be used to model legal processes as illustrated in the above sections. Our initial intuition was that using the primitive transaction patterns, legal service collaboration in courts processes could easily be modeled. With the utilization of the proposed transaction patterns in designing complex legal collaborations, much of burdens connected with specification of legal workflows could readily be overcome. Especially, as evident here, the identified primitive legal service transaction patterns are semantically rich enough for composing into complex multi-party collaborations in legal sector in selected Case Filling and Courts Hearing application areas.

Altogether, the applications of framework are resulted possibility of streamlining and then to ensure coordination among legal workflow activities in courts proceedings. These have the potential of achieving productivity and efficiency with promising results. It therefore is clear that the proposed transaction patterns can be used as basic building blocks in the process of constructing complex multi-party legal collaboration workflow models.

Further, we interacted with domain experts that we contacted during this work and able to understand the following points from the comments received. Legal personnel that we interacted with are aware the potential benefits of utilization of Information Technology (IT) in legal sector. However, due to the communication gap between technologists and legal experts, they even have some unpleasant experiences with attempts introduce IT solutions to meet the exact requirements. But, they are confident with these transaction patterns expressed in BPMN as a communication-bridge between technical teams and sector experts. Also with representation of legal processes using BPMN, we are formalizing the domain knowledge and providing a notion that is readily understandable by all sector participants, from the legal sector analysts that create the initial drafts of the processes, to the technical developers responsible for implementing the technology that will perform those processes, and finally, to the people who will manage and monitor those processes.

# 7

# Concluding Remarks and Future Directions

Effectiveness of the legal sector is highly relying on the coordination of workflow activities, as sector participants are initially dispersed around many geographical areas while acting on a same legal case. However, since WFMS have become an ideal tool for defining and managing the coordination of collaborative workflow activities, we have discovered the appropriateness of the adaption of WFMS in legal sector as well.

To the best of our knowledge, a proper investigation had not yet been conducted to develop the process models for legal WFMS. Therefore it is very important to engage in research work that fills this gap in the legal sector. These research contributions could be used as development assistant in the legal service solution developments.

In this work, we have proposed a sound framework for legal service collaboration modelling in such a way as to provide a useful input for the creation of legal workflow specifications for setting up legal WFMS. Taking current divorce case procedure in civil case category under districts court system in Sri Lanka as an example; we have studied the case workflow in order to get the domain understand. For the development of this framework, we have based a set of legal service transaction patterns aligned with globally accepted standard, UN/CEFACT's recommendations. UN/CEFACT recommends six standards transaction patterns for modeling trading collaboration that could be utilized in general business. However, during our investigation in legal sector we have experienced and realized significant differences between generic business trading procedures compared against to legal service collaborations. These differences resulted limitations on adopting the original UN/CEFACT's proposals as it is. However in this work, extensions have been proposed to UMM with the objective of accommodating demanding legal sector requirements while ensuring the alignment with UN/CE-FACT's recommendations.

Basically, the proposed framework could be considered as a set of methodological guidelines that support a designer to developed e-legal systems. When a developer builds up the systematic system for legal sector without any assistance from any methodological support, may encounter many hardships such as tackling complexity, correctness and completeness in relation to the system being developed. In this context, proposed pre-define set of transaction pattern could facilitate developers to model collaboration in the legal sector. With the utilization of these proposed transaction patterns in designing complex legal collaborations following promising benefits are achievable.

- Streamlined Legal Workflows - Complex Multi-party legal service collaborations have been realized through binary collaboration. With the formalization of these processes, productivity and efficiency are granted.

- Bridging Communication Gap - Often time a complaint that has been received by domain experts are the communication gap between technical and non-technical persons. However we have been seen this communication-gap been bridged with the proposed BPMN (high level) transaction patterns

- Bidirectional Traceability - With the utilization of a framework proposed here as an intermediate interface between requirements and implementation, downwards (from requirements to implementation) and upwards (from implementation to requirement) traceability can easily be achieved

- Adaptability - This proposed development has the facility of incorporating the expansions in the legal WFMS in future

- Scalability - The proposed development approach is the technology independent. That is developers can develop legal WFMS on any technological platform

Accordingly, with the utilization of the proposed transaction patterns in designing complex legal collaborations, much of burdens connected with specification of legal workflows in courts hearing procedure could readily be overcome. Especially, the identified primitive legal service transaction patterns are semantically rich enough for composing into complex multiparty collaborations in legal sector not only in selected application area in the paper but in many other areas of court proceedings. Therefore suggested future works include, complete evaluation on the selected application as well as in other possible areas of courts proceedings to carryout.

# Bibliography

[1] A Practical Guide to Research Methods: A user-friendly manual for mastering research techniques and projects, How to Books,2002.

[2] Business Process Management Initiative (BPMI), http://www.bpmi.org/, June 06,2014.

[3] Business Process Modelling Notation Specification (OMG),http://www.omg.org/spec/BPMN/2.0/, June 06,2014.

[4] Business Process Specification Schema (ebXML),http://www.ebxml.org/specs/ebBPSS.pdf, June 06,2014.

[5] Communication Environment for Judicial Network in Europe and Western Balkans,https://e-court.ca/legalT.pdf, June 06,2014.

[6] SecurE-Justice,http://www.rcc.gov.pt/SiteCollectionDocuments/SecurE-Justice_Italy.pdf, June 06,2014.

[7] The Workflow Management Coalition Specification,http://www.aiai.ed.ac.uk/project/wfmc/ARCHIVE/DOCS/refmodel/rmv1-16.html#, June 06,2014.

[8] UMM - User Guide,http://www.unece.org/cefact/umm/UMM_userguide_220606.pdf, June 06,2014.